PRO BASEBALL RECORDS

RECORDS

A GUIDE FOR EVERY FAN

BY MATT CHANDLER

COMPASS POINT BOOKS
a capstone imprint

Compass Point Books are published by Capstone
1710 Roe Crest Drive, North Mankato, Minnesota 56003
www.mycapstone.com

Editorial Credits

Lauren Dupuis-Perez, editor; Sara Radka, designer;
Eric Gohl, media researcher; Laura Manthe, production specialist

Library of Congress Cataloging-in-Publication Data
Library of Congress Cataloging-in-Publication data is available on the Library of Congress website.

ISBN 978-1-5435-5463-2 (library binding)
ISBN 978-1-5435-5935-4 (paperback)
ISBN 978-1-5435-5468-7 (eBook PDF)

Photo Credits

Getty Images: Abbie Parr, 15, Al Bello, 57 (top), Allsport, 51, Allsport/David Seelig, 56, Allsport/Ezra Shaw, 4, Allsport/Joe Patronite, 53 (bottom), Allsport/Jonathan Daniel, 49, Allsport/Matthew Stockman, 59, Allsport/Otto Greule, 43 (top), 46 (top), Allsport/Otto Greule Jr., 54 (top), Allsport/Stephen Dunn, 29 (bottom), Allsport/Todd Warshaw, 61 (bottom), Doug Pensinger, 17 (bottom), Drew Hallowell, 8, Eliot J. Schechter, 48, Elsa, 16 (top), 40, 54 (bottom), Ezra Shaw, 6, iStock, background, Jamie Squire, 32, Jayne Kamin-Oncea, 46 (bottom), Jed Jacobsohn, 7, Jonathan Daniel, 29 (top), 47 (top), Mike Ehrmann, 30, Otto Greule Jr, 11, 16 (bottom), Patrick Smith, 13, 57 (bottom), Rick Stewart, 45 (left), Rob Carr, 38, 41, 47 (bottom), Sean M. Haffey, 22, 45 (right), Stephen Dunn, 19; Newscom: AI Wire Photo Service, 35, Everett Collection, 26 (bottom), 42, SportsChrome KG, 14 (bottom); Pixabay: cindydangerjones, cover (field); Shutterstock: adike, cover (ball); Wikimedia: Apex Photo Company, 20, Bain News Service, 28, 53 (top), 58, Bowman Gum, 14 (top), Bowman Gum/Play Ball cards, 43 (bottom), Charles M Conlon, 27, George Grantham Bain Collection, 44, Goodwin & Co, 61 (top), 60, Irwin, La Broad, & Pudlin, 12, John Mena, 50, Library of Congress, 17 (top), 21, Louis Van Oeyen, 18, New York Yankees, 36, NYPL, 52, Paul Thompson, 26 (top), 55, The Sporting News, 9, Unknown, 10, 37

All stats are through the 2017 MLB season.

Printed in the United States of America.
PA49

Table of Contents

CHAPTER 1

Hitting 6

CHAPTER 2

Pitching 22

CHAPTER 3

Teams 32

CHAPTER 4

Postseason and All-Stars 38

CHAPTER 5

The Best and the Rest 42

Read More 62

Internet Sites 62

Index 63

IRON MAN

On May 30, 1982, 21,632 fans crowded into Baltimore's Memorial Stadium. They had no idea they were about to be part of history. Orioles rookie Cal Ripken Jr. jogged out and took his position at third base. It was a tough day for the kid. He went 0-2 at the plate with a strikeout and his team was shut out 6-0 by the visiting Toronto Blue Jays.

That game was the beginning of what many consider to be the most unreachable record in baseball. Ripken took the field the next night against the Texas Rangers, and every day and night for 2,632 consecutive games. Ripken played through batting slumps and injuries, never missing a game.

In 1939, Hall of Fame first baseman Lou Gehrig played in his 2,130th consecutive game. This created a record experts said would never be broken. More than 50 years later, Ripken did the seemingly impossible.

From Ripken's Iron Man streak to Barry Bonds' chase to take the home run crown from Hank Aaron, watching records be set and broken is part of what makes the game so exciting. But setting records takes more than skill. It takes good health, reliance on teammates, and sometimes a bit of luck to land in the record books.

Since Ripken took the field for his 2,632nd consecutive game, no player has even made it halfway to his record. Could the next Ripken be out there somewhere, playing in his first game of a record-breaking streak? Time will tell, as players, teams, and managers set their sights on earning a place in the record books of America's favorite pastime.

CHAPTER 1

Hitting

A stros second baseman Jose Altuve lit up American League pitchers in 2017. That year, he hit a league-leading .346. But Altuve failed to crack the top 10 in home runs or runs batted in (RBI). In the National League, Miami Marlins slugger Giancarlo Stanton had a monster year in 2017. He crushed 59 home runs and drove in 132 runs. But Stanton hit just .281, 24th in the National League in batting average.

Often a player can hit for a high average, but not for power. Or a player might hit a lot of home runs, but hit for a low average. Only 17 times in history has a player earned the triple crown.

This means he led the league in batting average, home runs, and RBI in the same season.

Miguel Cabrera was the last man to accomplish this rare hitting feat. He batted .330 for the Detroit Tigers in 2012 while launching 44 home runs and driving in 139. Cabrera captured the first triple crown since Red Sox leftfielder Carl Yastrzemski achieved the feat in 1967. Since then, many players have led the league in two out of three categories. But until Cabrera put together his magical season, no one had put all three jewels in the triple crown for more than three decades.

● PLAYER RECORDS

Home Runs

CAREER

1	Barry Bonds	762	Pirates/Giants	1986–2007
2	Hank Aaron	755	Braves/Brewers	1954–1976
3	Babe Ruth	714	Red Sox/Yankees/Braves	1914–1935
4	Alex Rodriguez	696	Mariners/Rangers/Yankees	1994–2013, 2015–2016
5	Willie Mays	660	Giants/Mets	1951–52, 1954–1973
6	Ken Griffey Jr.	630	Mariners/Reds/White Sox	1989–2010
7	Albert Pujols	614	Cardinals/Angels	2001–2017*
8	Jim Thome	612	Indians/Phillies/White Sox/Dodgers/Twins/Orioles	1991–2012
9	Sammy Sosa	609	Rangers/White Sox/Cubs/Orioles	1989–2005, 2007
10	Frank Robinson	586	Reds/Orioles/Dodgers/Angels/Indians	1956–1976

SINGLE SEASON

1	Barry Bonds	73	Giants	2001
2	Mark McGwire	70	Cardinals	1998
3	Sammy Sosa	66	Cubs	1998
4	Mark McGwire	65	Cardinals	1999
5	Sammy Sosa	64	Cubs	2001
6	Sammy Sosa	63	Cubs	1999
7	Roger Maris	61	Yankees	1961
8	Babe Ruth	60	Yankees	1927
9	Babe Ruth	59	Yankees	1921
	Giancarlo Stanton	59	Marlins	2017*

▲ Barry Bonds

active player

Grand Slams

▲ Alex Rodriguez

CAREER

1	Alex Rodriguez	25	Mariners/Rangers/Yankees	1994–2013, 2015–2016
2	Lou Gehrig	23	Yankees	1923–1939
3	Manny Ramirez	21	Indians/Red Sox/Dodgers/White Sox/Rays	1993–2011
4	Eddie Murray	19	Orioles/Dodgers/Mets/Indians/Angels	1977–1997
5	Willie McCovey	18	Giants/Padres/Athletics	1959–1980
	Robin Ventura	18	White Sox/Mets/Yankees/Dodgers	1989–2004
7	Jimmie Foxx	17	Athletics/Red Sox/Cubs/Phillies	1925–1945
	Ted Williams	17	Red Sox	1939–1942, 1946–1960
	Carlos Lee	17	White Sox/Brewers/Rangers/Astros/Marlins	1999–2012
10	Three players tied with 16			

SINGLE SEASON

1	Don Mattingly	6	Yankees	1987
	Travis Hafner	6	Indians	2006
3	Ernie Banks	5	Cubs	1955
	Jim Gentile	5	Orioles	1961
	Richie Sexson	5	Mariners	2006
	Albert Pujols	5	Cardinals	2009*
7	Many players tied with 4			

*active player

RECORD FACT

Pete Milne hit an inside-the-park grand slam on April 27, 1949. It was the only home run of his major league career.

Inside-the-Park Home Runs

CAREER

1	**Jesse Burkett**	55	Giants/Spiders/Perfectos/Cardinals/Browns/Americans	1890–1905
2	**Sam Crawford**	51	Reds/Tigers	1899–1917
3	**Tommy Leach**	48	Colonels/Pirates/Cubs/Reds	1898–1915, 1918
4	**Ty Cobb**	46	Tigers/Athletics	1895–1928
	Honus Wagner	46	Colonels/Pirates	1897–1917
6	**Jake Beckley**	38	Alleghenys/Burghers/Pirates/Giants/Reds/Cardinals	1888–1907
	Tris Speaker	38	Americans/Red Sox/Indians/Senators/Athletics	1907–1928
8	**Rogers Hornsby**	33	Cardinals/Giants/Braves/Cubs/Browns	1915–1937
9	**Edd Roush**	31	White Sox/Hoosiers/Pepper/Giants/Reds	1913–1929, 1931
10	**Willie Keeler**	30	Giants/Grooms/Orioles/Superbas/Highlanders	1892–1910
	Jake Daubert	30	Superbas/Dodgers/Robins/Reds	1910–1924

▲ Jesse Burkett

RECORD FACT

Ichiro Suzuki is the only player in history to hit an inside-the-park home run in an All-Star Game. In the 2007 contest at AT&T Park in San Francisco, he drove a ball to right center field that took a crazy bounce off the wall. Ichiro scored standing up for a two-run homer.

Batting Average

▲ Rogers Hornsby

CAREER

1	Ty Cobb	.366	Tigers/Athletics	1905–1928
2	Rogers Hornsby	.359	Cardinals/Giants/Braves/Cubs/Browns	1915–1937
3	Joe Jackson	.356	Athletics/Naps/Indians/White Sox	1908–1920
4	Lefty O'Doul	.349	Yankees/Red Sox/Giants/Phillies/Robins/Dodgers	1919–1920, 1922–23, 1928–1934
5	Ed Delahanty	.346	Quakers/Infants/Phillies/Senators	1888–1903
6	Tris Speaker	.345	Americans/Red Sox/Indians/Senators/Athletics	1907–1928
7	Billy Hamilton	.344	Cowboys/Phillies/Beaneaters	1888–1901
	Ted Williams	.344	Red Sox	1939–1942, 1946–1960
9	Dan Brouthers	.342	Trojans/Bisons/Wolverines/Beaneaters/Reds/Grooms/Orioles/Colonels/Phillies/Giants	1879–1896, 1904
	Babe Ruth	.342	Red Sox/Yankees/Braves	1914–1935

SINGLE SEASON

1	Hugh Duffy	.440	Beaneaters	1894
2	Tip O'Neill	.435	Browns	1887
3	Ross Barnes	.429	White Stockings	1876
4	Nap Lajoie	.427	Athletics	1901
5	Willie Keeler	.424	Orioles	1897
	Rogers Hornsby	.424	Cardinals	1924
7	Ty Cobb	.420	Tigers	1911
	George Sisler	.420	Browns	1922
9	Tuck Turner	.418	Phillies	1894
10	Sam Thompson	.415	Phillies	1894

Runs Scored

CAREER

1	**Rickey Henderson**	2,295	Athletics/Yankees/Blue Jays/Padres/Angels/Mets/Mariners/Red Sox/Dodgers	1979–2003
2	**Ty Cobb**	2,244	Tigers/Athletics	1905–1928
3	**Barry Bonds**	2,227	Pirates/Giants	1986–2007
4	**Babe Ruth**	2,174	Red Sox/Yankees/Braves	1914–1935
	Hank Aaron	2,174	Braves/Brewers	1954–1976
6	**Pete Rose**	2,165	Reds/Phillies/Expos	1963–1986
7	**Willie Mays**	2,062	Giants/Mets	1951–1952, 1954–1973
8	**Alex Rodriguez**	2,021	Mariners/Rangers/Yankees	1994–2013, 2015–2016
9	**Cap Anson**	1,999	Forest Citys/Athletics/White Stockings/Colts	1871–1897
10	**Stan Musial**	1,949	Cardinals	1941–1944, 1946–1963

▲ Rickey Henderson

SINGLE SEASON

1	**Billy Hamilton**	198	Phillies	1894
2	**Tom Brown**	177	Reds	1891
	Babe Ruth	177	Yankees	1921
4	**Tip O'Neill**	167	Browns	1887
	Lou Gehrig	167	Yankees	1936
6	**Billy Hamilton**	166	Phillies	1895
7	**Willie Keeler**	165	Orioles	1894
	Joe Kelley	165	Orioles	1894
9	**Arlie Latham**	163	Browns	1887
	Babe Ruth	163	Yankees	1928
	Lou Gehrig	163	Yankees	1931

Runs Batted In

CAREER

1	**Hank Aaron**	2,297	Braves/Brewers	1954–1976
2	**Babe Ruth**	2,214	Red Sox/Yankees/Braves	1914–1935
3	**Alex Rodriguez**	2,086	Mariners/Rangers/Yankees	1994–2013, 2015–2016
4	**Cap Anson**	2,075	Forest Citys/Athletics/ White Stockings/Colts	1871–1897
5	**Barry Bonds**	1,996	Pirates/Giants	1986–2007
6	**Lou Gehrig**	1,995	Yankees	1923–1939
7	**Stan Musial**	1,951	Cardinals	1941–1944, 1946–1963
8	**Ty Cobb**	1,938	Tigers/Athletics	1905–1928
9	**Jimmie Foxx**	1,922	Athletics/Red Sox/Cubs/Phillies	1925–1945
10	**Albert Pujols**	1,918	Cardinals/Angels	2001–2017*

active player

SINGLE SEASON

1	**Hack Wilson**	191	Cubs	1930
2	**Lou Gehrig**	185	Yankees	1931
3	**Hank Greenberg**	184	Tigers	1937
4	**Jimmie Foxx**	175	Red Sox	1938
5	**Lou Gehrig**	173	Yankees	1927
	Lou Gehrig	173	Yankees	1930
7	**Chuck Klein**	170	Phillies	1930
8	**Jimmie Foxx**	169	Athletics	1932
9	**Babe Ruth**	168	Yankees	1921
	Hank Greenberg	168	Tigers	1935

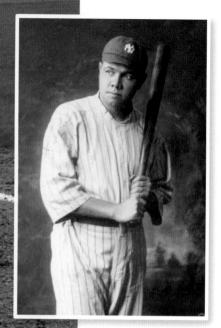

▲ Babe Ruth

SINGLE GAME

1	Jim Bottomley	12	Cardinals	1924
	Mark Whiten	12	Cardinals	1993
3	Wilbert Robinson	11	Orioles	1892
	Tony Lazzeri	11	Yankees	1936
	Phil Weintraub	11	Giants	1944
6	Eleven players tied with 10			

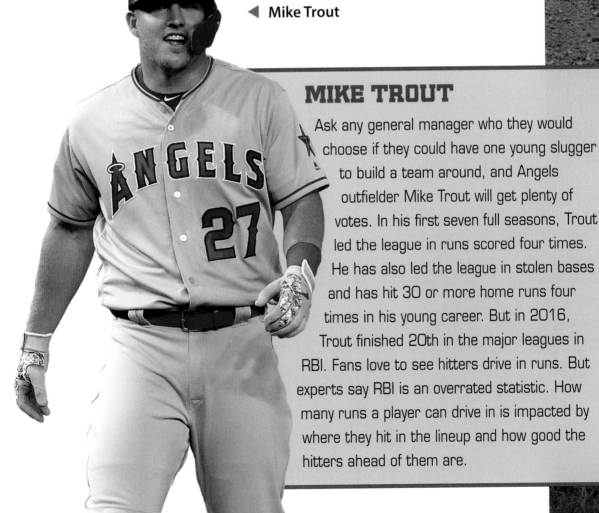

◀ Mike Trout

MIKE TROUT

Ask any general manager who they would choose if they could have one young slugger to build a team around, and Angels outfielder Mike Trout will get plenty of votes. In his first seven full seasons, Trout led the league in runs scored four times. He has also led the league in stolen bases and has hit 30 or more home runs four times in his young career. But in 2016, Trout finished 20th in the major leagues in RBI. Fans love to see hitters drive in runs. But experts say RBI is an overrated statistic. How many runs a player can drive in is impacted by where they hit in the lineup and how good the hitters ahead of them are.

Hits

▲ Stan Musial

CAREER

1	**Pete Rose**	4,256	Reds/Phillies/Expos	1963–1986
2	**Ty Cobb**	4,189	Tigers/Athletics	1905–1928
3	**Hank Aaron**	3,771	Braves/Brewers	1954–1976
4	**Stan Musial**	3,630	Cardinals	1941–1944, 1946–1963
5	**Tris Speaker**	3,514	Americans/Red Sox/ Indians/Senators/ Athletics	1907–1928
6	**Derek Jeter**	3,465	Yankees	1995–2014
7	**Cap Anson**	3,435	Forest Citys/Athletics/ White Stockings/Colts	1871–1897
8	**Honus Wagner**	3,420	Colonels/Pirates	1897–1917
9	**Carl Yastrzemski**	3,419	Red Sox	1961–1983
10	**Paul Molitor**	3,319	Brewers/Blue Jays/Twins	1978–1998

▲ Pete Rose

RECORD FACT

Pete Rose became baseball's all-time hits leader on September 11, 1985. He singled to left center field off of San Diego Padres pitcher Eric Show. Rose was both a player for the Cincinnati Reds and the manager of the team when he broke the record.

SINGLE SEASON

1	**Ichiro Suzuki**	262	Mariners	2004*
2	**George Sisler**	257	Browns	1920
3	**Lefty O'Doul**	254	Phillies	1929
	Bill Terry	254	Giants	1930
5	**Al Simmons**	253	Athletics	1925
6	**Rogers Hornsby**	250	Cardinals	1922
	Chuck Klein	250	Phillies	1930
8	**Ty Cobb**	248	Tigers	1911
9	**George Sisler**	246	Browns	1922
10	**Ichiro Suzuki**	242	Mariners	2001*

active player

▲ Ichiro Suzuki

Singles

CAREER

1	Pete Rose	3,215	Reds/Phillies/Expos	1963–1986
2	Ty Cobb	3,053	Tigers/Athletics	1905–1928
3	Eddie Collins	2,643	Athletics/White Sox	1906–1930
4	Cap Anson	2,614	Forest Citys/Athletics/White Stockings/Colts	1871–1897
5	Derek Jeter	2,595	Yankees	1995–2014
6	Ichiro Suzuki	2,505	Mariners/Yankees/Marlins	2001–2017*
7	Willie Keeler	2,513	Giants/Grooms/Orioles/Superbas/Highlanders	1892–1910
8	Honus Wagner	2,424	Colonels/Pirates	1897–1917
9	Rod Carew	2,404	Twins/Angels	1967–1985
10	Tris Speaker	2,383	Americans/Red Sox/Indians/Senators/Athletics	1907–1928

▲ Derek Jeter

▲ Wade Boggs

SINGLE SEASON

1	Ichiro Suzuki	225	Mariners	2004*
2	Willie Keller	206	Orioles	1898
3	Ichiro Suzuki	203	Mariners	2007*
4	Lloyd Waner	198	Pirates	1927
5	Willie Keeler	193	Orioles	1897
6	Ichiro Suzuki	192	Mariners	2001*
7	Jesse Burkett	191	Spiders	1896
8	Willie Keeler	190	Superbas	1899
9	Wade Boggs	187	Red Sox	1985
10	Jesse Burkett	186	Spiders	1898

active player

Doubles

CAREER

1	**Tris Speaker**	792	Americans/Red Sox/Indians/ Senators/Athletics	1907–1928
2	**Pete Rose**	746	Reds/Phillies/Expos	1963–1986
3	**Stan Musial**	725	Cardinals	1941–1944, 1946–1963
4	**Ty Cobb**	724	Tigers/Athletics	1905–1928
5	**Craig Biggio**	668	Astros	1988–2007
6	**George Brett**	665	Royals	1973–1993
6	**Nap Lajoie**	657	Phillies/Athletics/ Bronchos/Naps	1896–1916
8	**Carl Yastrzemski**	646	Red Sox	1961–1983
9	**Honus Wagner**	643	Colonels/Pirates	1897–1917
10	**David Ortiz**	632	Twins/Red Sox	1997–2016

▲ Tris Speaker

SINGLE SEASON

1	**Earl Webb**	67	Red Sox	1931
2	**George Burns**	64	Indians	1926
	Joe Medwick	64	Cardinals	1936
4	**Hank Greenberg**	63	Tigers	1934
5	**Paul Waner**	62	Pirates	1932
6	**Charlie Gehringer**	60	Tigers	1936
7	**Tris Speaker**	59	Indians	1923
	Chuck Klein	59	Phillies	1930
	Todd Helton	59	Rockies	2000
10	**Billy Herman**	57	Cubs	1935
	Billy Herman	57	Cubs	1936
	Carlos Delgado	57	Blue Jays	2000

▲ Todd Helton

Triples

CAREER

1	**Sam Crawford**	309	Reds/Tigers	1899–1917
2	**Ty Cobb**	295	Tigers/Athletics	1905–1928
3	**Honus Wagner**	252	Colonels/Pirates	1897–1917
4	**Jake Beckley**	244	Alleghenys/Burghers/Pirates/ Giants/Reds/Cardinals	1888–1907
5	**Roger Connor**	233	Trojans/Gothams/Giants/ Phillies/Browns	1880–1897
6	**Tris Speaker**	222	Americans/Red Sox/Indians/ Senators/Athletics	1907–1928
7	**Fred Clarke**	220	Colonels/Pirates	1894–1911, 1913–1915
8	**Dan Brouthers**	205	Trojans/Bisons/ Wolverines/Beaneaters/ Reds/Grooms/Orioles/ Colonels/Phillies/Giants	1879–1904
9	**Joe Kelley**	194	Beaneaters/Pirates/Orioles/ Superbas/Reds/Doves	1891–1906, 1908
10	**Paul Waner**	191	Pirates/Dodgers/ Braves/Yankees	1926–1945

▲ Ty Cobb

SINGLE SEASON

1	**Chief Wilson**	36	Pirates	1912
2	**Dave Orr**	31	Metropolitans	1886
	Heinie Reitz	31	Orioles	1894
4	**Perry Werden**	29	Browns	1893
5	**Sam Thompson**	28	Phillies	1894
	Harry Davis	28	Pirates	1897
7	**George Davis**	27	Giants	1893
	Jimmy Williams	27	Pirates	1899
9	**Five players tied with 26**			

Stolen Bases

CAREER

1	**Rickey Henderson**	1,406	Athletics/Yankees/Blue Jays/Padres/Angels/Mets/Mariners/Red Sox/Dodgers	1979–2003
2	**Lou Brock**	938	Cubs/Cardinals	1961–1979
3	**Billy Hamilton**	914	Cowboys/Phillies/Beaneaters	1888–1901
4	**Ty Cobb**	897	Tigers/Athletics	1905–1928
5	**Tim Raines**	808	Expos/White Sox/Yankees/Athletics/Orioles/Marlins	1979–1999, 2001–2002
6	**Vince Coleman**	752	Cardinals/Mets/Royals/Mariners/Reds/Tigers	1985–1997
7	**Arlie Latham**	742	Bisons/Browns/Pirates/Reds/Senators/Giants	1880, 1883–1896, 1899, 1909
8	**Eddie Collins**	741	Athletics/White Sox	1906–1930
9	**Max Carey**	738	Pirates/Robins	1910–1929
10	**Honus Wagner**	723	Colonels/Pirates	1897–1917

SINGLE SEASON

1	**Hugh Nicol**	138	Red Stockings	1887
2	**Rickey Henderson**	130	Athletics	1982
3	**Arlie Latham**	129	Browns	1887
4	**Lou Brock**	118	Cardinals	1974
5	**Charlie Comiskey**	117	Browns	1887
6	**John Ward**	111	Giants	1887
	Billy Hamilton	111	Cowboys	1889
	Billy Hamilton	111	Phillies	1891
9	**Vince Coleman**	110	Cardinals	1985
10	**Arlie Latham**	109	Browns	1888
	Vince Coleman	109	Cardinals	1987

▲ Lou Brock

Walks

CAREER

1	Barry Bonds	2,558	Pirates/Giants	1986–2007
2	Rickey Henderson	2,190	Athletics/Yankees/Blue Jays/Padres/Angels/Mets/Mariners/Red Sox/Dodgers	1979–2003
3	Babe Ruth	2,062	Red Sox/Yankees/Braves	1914–1935
4	Ted Williams	2,021	Red Sox	1939–1942, 1946–1960
5	Joe Morgan	1,865	Colt .45s/Astros/Reds/Giants/Phillies/Athletics	1963–1984
6	Carl Yastrzemski	1,845	Red Sox	1961–1983
7	Jim Thome	1,747	Indians/Phillies/White Sox/Dodgers/Twins/Orioles	1991–2012
8	Mickey Mantle	1,733	Yankees	1951–1968
9	Mel Ott	1,708	Giants	1926–1947
10	Frank Thomas	1,667	White Sox/Athletics/Blue Jays	1990–2008

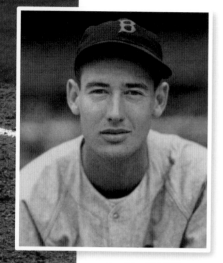

▲ Ted Williams

SINGLE SEASON

1	Barry Bonds	232	Giants	2004
2	Barry Bonds	198	Giants	2002
3	Barry Bonds	177	Giants	2001
4	Babe Ruth	170	Yankees	1923
5	Ted Williams	162	Red Sox	1947
	Ted Williams	162	Red Sox	1949
	Mark McGwire	162	Cardinals	1998
8	Ted Williams	156	Red Sox	1946
9	Eddie Yost	151	Senators	1956
	Barry Bonds	151	Giants	1996

RECORD FACT

Nationals outfielder Bryce Harper is the only player in major league history to reach base seven times in a single game without recording an official at bat. Harper walked six times and was hit by a pitch in a game against the Chicago Cubs on May 8, 2016.

Hit By Pitch

CAREER

1	**Hughie Jennings**	287	Colonels/Orioles/ Superbas/ Phillies/Tigers	1891–1903, 1907, 1909–1910, 1912, 1918
2	**Craig Biggio**	285	Astros	1988–2007
3	**Tommy Tucker**	272	Orioles/Beaneaters/ Senators/Bridegrooms/ Browns/Spiders	1887–1899
4	**Don Baylor**	267	Orioles/Athletics/ Angels/Yankees/ Red Sox/Twins	1970–1988
5	**Jason Kendall**	254	Pirates/Athletics/ Cubs/Brewers/Royals	1996–2010
6	**Ron Hunt**	243	Mets/Dodgers/Giants/ Expos/Cardinals	1963–1974
7	**Dan McGann**	230	Beaneaters/Orioles/ Superbas/Senators/ Cardinals/Giants/Doves	1896, 1898–1908
8	**Chase Utley**	199	Phillies/Dodgers	2003–2017*
9	**Frank Robinson**	198	Redlegs/Reds/ Orioles/Dodgers/ Angels/Indians	1956–1976
10	**Minnie Minoso**	192	Indians/White Sox/ Cardinals/Senators	1949, 1951–1964, 1976, 1980

* active player

▲ **Hughie Jennings**

RECORD FACT

The longest at-bat in MLB history came on April 22, 2018. San Francisco Giants first baseman Brandon Belt faced 21 pitches in an at-bat that lasted almost 13 minutes! Belt fouled off 11 straight pitches during the at-bat against Angels pitcher Jaime Barria before eventually flying out to right field.

CHAPTER 2
Pitching

On June 18, 2014, Clayton Kershaw took the mound in front of his Los Angeles Dodgers home crowd. He completely dominated the Colorado Rockies, tossing the 22nd no-hitter in team history.

Kershaw was in the zone all night. He struck out 15 batters and walked none. When the pressure was the greatest, in the last two innings, the "Claw" didn't throw a single ball out of the strike zone.

Kershaw's night was almost perfect. Shortstop Hanley Ramirez made a throwing error, allowing one Rockies player to reach base. If Ramirez had made the throw, Kershaw would have joined an even more elite group. There have only been 23 perfect games recorded in major league history. No walks, no hit batters, no hits, and no errors with 27 consecutive outs. It is the pinnacle of success for a pitcher, and Kershaw was one play from perfection.

There have been only 23 perfect games in more than 140 seasons. Strangely, there were three perfect games in 2012 alone. It is the only season in history with three perfect games. There hasn't been one since.

PITCHING RECORDS

Wins

CAREER

1	**Cy Young**	511	Spiders/Perfectos/Cardinals/Americans/Naps/Rustlers/Red Sox	1890–1911
2	**Walter Johnson**	417	Senators	1907–1927
3	**Christy Mathewson**	373	Giants/Reds	1900–1916
	Grover Alexander	373	Phillies/Cubs/Cardinals	1911–1930
5	**Pud Galvin**	365	Brown Stockings/Bisons/Alleghenys/Burghers/Pirates/Browns	1875, 1879–1892
6	**Warren Spahn**	363	Braves/Mets/Giants	1942, 1946–1965
7	**Kid Nichols**	361	Beaneaters/Cardinals/Phillies	1890–1901, 1904–1906
8	**Greg Maddux**	355	Cubs/Braves/Dodgers/Padres	1986–2008
9	**Roger Clemens**	354	Red Sox/Blue Jays/Yankees/Astros	1984–2007
10	**Tim Keefe**	342	Trojans/Metropolitans/Giants/Phillies	1880–1893

SINGLE SEASON

1	**Charles "Old Hoss" Radbourn**	59	Grays	1884
2	**John Clarkson**	53	White Stockings	1885
3	**Guy Hecker**	52	Eclipse	1884
4	**John Clarkson**	49	Beaneaters	1889
5	**Charles "Old Hoss" Radbourn**	48	Grays	1883
	Charlie Buffinton	48	Beaneaters	1884
7	**Al Spaulding**	47	White Stockings	1876
	John Ward	47	Grays	1879
9	**Pud Galvin**	46	Bisons	1883
	Pud Galvin	46	Bisons	1884
	Matt Kilroy	46	Orioles	1887

Strikeouts

CAREER

1	Nolan Ryan	5,714	Mets/Angels/Astros/Rangers	1966, 1968–1993
2	Randy Johnson	4,875	Expos/Mariners/Astros/Diamondbacks/Yankees/Giants	1988–2009
3	Roger Clemens	4,672	Red Sox/Blue Jays/Yankees/Astros	1984–2007
4	Steve Carlton	4,136	Cardinals/Phillies/Giants/White Sox/Indians/Twins	1965–1988
5	Bert Blyleven	3,701	Twins/Rangers/Pirates/Indians/Angels	1970–1990, 1992
6	Tom Seaver	3,640	Mets/Reds/White Sox/Red Sox	1967–1986
7	Don Sutton	3,574	Dodgers/Astros/Brewers/Athletics/Angels	1966–1988
8	Gaylord Perry	3,534	Giants/Indians/Rangers/Padres/Yankees/Braves/Mariners/Royals	1962–1983
9	Walter Johnson	3,509	Senators	1907–1927
10	Greg Maddux	3,371	Cubs/Braves/Dodgers/Padres	1986–2008

SINGLE SEASON

1	Matt Kilroy	513	Orioles	1886
2	Toad Ramsey	499	Colonels	1886
3	Hugh Daily	483	Chicago/Pittsburgh/Nationals	1884
4	Dupee Shaw	451	Wolverines/Reds	1884
5	Charles "Old Hoss" Radbourn	441	Grays	1884
6	Charlie Buffington	417	Beaneaters	1884
7	Guy Hecker	385	Eclipse	1884
8	Nolan Ryan	383	Angels	1973
9	Sandy Koufax	382	Dodgers	1965
10	Bill Sweeney	374	Monumentals	1884

Innings Pitched

CAREER

1	**Cy Young**	7,356	Spiders/Perfectos/Cardinals/Americans/Naps/Rustlers/Red Sox	1890–1911
2	**Pud Galvin**	6,003.1	Brown Stockings/Bisons/Alleghenys/Burghers/Pirates/Browns	1875, 1879–1892
3	**Walter Johnson**	5,914.1	Senators	1907–1927
4	**Phil Niekro**	5,404	Braves/Yankees/Indians/Blue Jays	1964–1987
5	**Nolan Ryan**	5,386	Mets/Angels/Astros/Rangers	1966, 1968–1993
6	**Gaylord Perry**	5,350	Giants/Indians/Rangers/Padres/Yankees/Braves/Mariners/Royals	1962–1983
7	**Don Sutton**	5,282.1	Dodgers/Astros/Brewers/Athletics/Angels	1966–1988
8	**Warren Spahn**	5,243.2	Braves/Mets/Giants	1942, 1946–1965
9	**Steve Carlton**	5,217.2	Cardinals/Phillies/Giants/White Sox/Indians/Twins	1965–1988
10	**Grover Alexander**	5,190	Phillies/Cubs/Cardinals	1911–1930

SINGLE SEASON

1	**Will White**	680	Reds	1879
2	**Charles "Old Hoss" Radbourn**	678.2	Grays	1884
3	**Guy Hecker**	670.2	Eclipse	1884
4	**Jim McCormick**	657.2	Blues	1880
5	**Pud Galvin**	656.1	Bisons	1883
6	**Pud Galvin**	636.1	Bisons	1884
7	**Charles "Old Hoss" Radbourn**	632.1	Grays	1883
8	**John Clarkson**	623	White Stockings	1885
9	**Jim Devlin**	622	Grays	1876
10	**Bill Hutchinson**	622	Colts	1892

Earned Run Average [ERA]

CAREER

1	**Ed Walsh**	1.82	White Sox/Braves	1904–1917
2	**Addie Joss**	1.89	Bronchos/Naps	1902–1910
3	**Jim Devlin**	1.90	White Stockings/Grays	1875–1877
4	**Jack Pfiester**	2.02	Pirates/Cubs	1903–1904, 1906–1911
5	**Joe Wood**	2.03	Red Sox/Indians	1908–1915, 1917, 1919–1920
6	**Mordecai Brown**	2.06	Cardinals/Cubs/Reds/ Terriers/Tip-Tops/Whales	1903–1916
7	**John Ward**	2.10	Grays/Gothams/Giants/ Wonders/Grooms	1878–1884
8	**Al Spalding**	2.13	Red Stockings/ White Stockings	1871–1877
	Christy Mathewson	2.13	Giants/Reds	1900–1916
10	**Tommy Bond**	2.14	Atlantics/Dark Blues/ Red Stockings/Ruby Legs/Reds/Hoosiers	1874–1882, 1884

▲ Ed Walsh

WORLD SERIES PERFECTION

It takes incredible talent, skill, timing, and a bit of luck to throw a perfect game. To do it under the bright lights and intense pressure of the World Series seems impossible. But in Game 5 of the 1956 World Series, Yankees pitcher Don Larsen was perfect. Larsen shut down the Brooklyn Dodgers, leading the Yankees to a 2-0 win. His team went on to win the series and Larsen was named MVP. It remains the only perfect game in postseason history.

▲ Don Larsen

Earned Run Average [ERA]

SINGLE SEASON

1	**Tim Keefe**	0.86	Trojans	1880
2	**Dutch Leonard**	0.96	Red Sox	1914
3	**Mordecai Brown**	1.04	Cubs	1906
4	**Bob Gibson**	1.12	Cardinals	1968
5	**Christy Mathewson**	1.14	Giants	1909
	Walter Johnson	1.14	Senators	1913
7	**Jack Pfiester**	1.15	Cubs	1907
8	**Addie Joss**	1.16	Naps	1908
9	**Carl Lundgren**	1.17	Cubs	1907
10	**Denny Driscoll**	1.21	Alleghenys	1882

RECORD FACT

Philadelphia Phillies pitcher Roy Halladay threw a no-hitter in his first postseason appearance, in the 2010 National League Division Series. Halladay also pitched a perfect game during the 2010 regular season.

▲ Walter Johnson

Shutouts

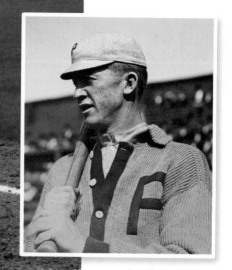

▲ Grover Alexander

CAREER

#	Player		Teams	Years
1	Walter Johnson	110	Senators	1907–1927
2	Grover Alexander	90	Phillies/Cubs/Cardinals	1911–1930
3	Christy Mathewson	79	Giants/Reds	1900–1916
4	Cy Young	76	Spiders/Perfectos/Cardinals/Americans/Naps/Rustlers/Red Sox	1890–1911
5	Eddie Plank	69	Athletics/Terriers/Browns	1901–1917
6	Warren Spahn	63	Braves/Mets/Giants	1942, 1946–1965
7	Nolan Ryan	61	Mets/Angels/Astros/Rangers	1966, 1968–1993
	Tom Seaver	61	Mets/Reds/White Sox/Red Sox	1967–1986
9	Bert Blyleven	60	Twins/Rangers/Pirates/Indians/Angels	1970–1990, 1992
10	Don Sutton	58	Dodgers/Astros/Brewers/Athletics/Angels	1966–1988

SINGLE SEASON

#	Player		Team	Year
1	George Bradley	16	Brown Stockings	1876
	Grover Alexander	16	Phillies	1916
3	Jack Coombs	13	Athletics	1910
	Bob Gibson	13	Cardinals	1968
5	Pud Galvin	12	Bisons	1884
	Ed Morris	12	Alleghenys	1886
	Grover Alexander	12	Phillies	1915
8	Eight players tied with 11 shutouts			

RECORD FACT

In 1988, Los Angeles Dodgers pitcher Orel Hershiser set the record for consecutive scoreless innings. Hershiser pitched 59 straight innings without allowing a run. He went on to lead the Dodgers to the World Series championship and was named World Series MVP.

CONSECUTIVE SHUTOUT INNINGS PITCHED

1	Orel Hershiser	59.0	Dodgers	1988
2	Don Drysdale	58.2	Dodgers	1968
3	Walter Johnson	55.2	Senators	1913
4	Jack Coombs	53.0	Athletics	1910
5	Bob Gibson	47.0	Cardinals	1968
6	Zack Greinke	45.2	Dodgers	2015
7	Carl Hubbell	45.1	Giants	1933
8	Doc White	45.0	White Sox	1904
	Cy Young	45.0	Red Sox	1904
	Sal Maglie	45.0	Giants	1950

▲ Orel Hershiser

LOTS OF LOSSES

Former Mets pitcher Anthony Young holds the record for most consecutive losses by a pitcher. Young lost 27 straight decisions between the 1992 and 1993 seasons. When the Mets rallied to earn Young a win and break the streak, he said, "That wasn't even a big monkey that was on my back, it was a zoo." Over the two seasons, Young had a combined record of 3-30.

◀ Anthony Young

Cy Young Winners

CAREER

1	Roger Clemens	7
2	Randy Johnson	5
3	Steve Carlton	4
	Greg Maddux	4
5	Clayton Kershaw	3
	Sandy Koufax	3
	Pedro Martinez	3
	Jim Palmer	3
	Tom Seaver	3
	Max Scherzer	3
11	Many players tied with 2	

GOING, GOING, GONE

Southpaw journeyman pitcher Jamie Moyer played for eight teams during his 25-year major league career. His longevity left him with one record he would rather forget. Moyer gave up 522 home runs in his career, the most all-time.

Twins ace Bert Blyleven led the American League in surrendered home runs in back-to-back seasons. This included setting the major league record when he gave up 50 long balls in 1986. Despite the unfortunate record, Blyleven was inducted into the National Baseball Hall of Fame in 2011. It was his 14th year on the ballot. Blyleven was finally elected, in part, thanks to the increased reliance on sabermetrics to evaluate players beyond traditional statistical measurements.

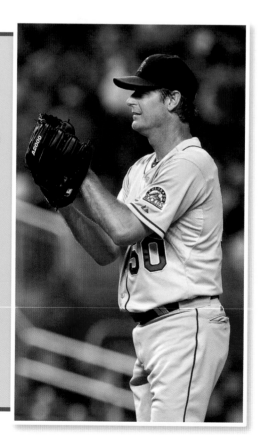

▲ Jamie Moyer

Saves

CAREER

1	**Mariano Rivera**	652	Yankees	1995–2013
2	**Trevor Hoffman**	601	Padres/Marlins/Brewers	1993–2010
3	**Lee Smith**	478	Cubs/Red Sox/Cardinals/Yankees/ Orioles/Angels/Red/Expos	1980–1997
4	**Francisco Rodriguez**	437	Angels/Mets/Brewers/Orioles/Tigers	2002–2017
5	**John Franco**	424	Mets/Reds/Astros	1984–2001, 2003–2005
6	**Billy Wagner**	422	Astros/Phillies/Mets/Red Sox/Braves	1995–2010
7	**Dennis Eckersley**	390	Indians/Red Sox/Cubs/Athletics/Cardinals	1975–1998
8	**Joe Nathan**	377	Giants/Twins/Rangers/Tigers/Cubs	1999–2000, 2002–2009, 2011–2016
9	**Jonathan Papelbon**	368	Red Sox/Phillies/Nationals	2005–2016
10	**Jeff Reardon**	367	Mets/Expos/Twins/Red Sox/ Braves/Reds/Yankees	1979–1994

SINGLE SEASON

1	**Francisco Rodriguez**	62	Angels	2008
2	**Bobby Thigpen**	57	White Sox	1990
3	**John Smoltz**	55	Braves	2002
	Eric Gagne	55	Dodgers	2003
5	**Randy Myers**	53	Cubs	1993
	Trevor Hoffman	53	Padres	1998
	Mariano Rivera	53	Yankees	2004
8	**Eric Gagne**	52	Dodgers	2002
9	**Five players tied with 51 saves**			

CHAPTER 3

Teams

No team has been as dominant as the New York Yankees. The "Bronx Bombers" have won 27 World Series titles, 16 more than the next-closest team. They also have the highest winning percentage in the history of the game. Many of the all-time greats—Ruth, DiMaggio, Gehrig, Mantle, and Maris—all wore Yankee pinstripes.

The Boston Red Sox may not have as many rings as their biggest rival. But as one of the oldest teams in baseball, the Red Sox have been dominant in their own right. The Red Sox won three World Series crowns in a four-year stretch from 1915 to 1918. After an 86-year drought, the Sox swept the St. Louis Cardinals to win the 2004 World Series.

Despite being swept by the Red Sox in 2004 and losing the 2013 World Series to Boston, no team has come closer to the Yankees' greatness than the St. Louis Cardinals. With 23 National League pennants (4 as the Browns and 19 as the Cardinals) and 11 World Series titles, the Cardinals have proven to be a baseball dynasty. The Cardinals have won World Series titles in eight different decades, one of those as the Browns. Their rivalry with the Chicago Cubs has been one of the best in baseball.

Win-Loss Percentage [Best]

FRANCHISE HISTORY

1	New York Yankees	56.9	10,175–7,719
2	San Francisco Giants	53.7	11,015–9,513
3	Los Angeles Dodgers	52.7	10,776–9,691
4	St. Louis Cardinals	52.0	10,739–9,918
5	Boston Red Sox	51.7	9,410–8,776
6	Chicago Cubs	51.3	10,803–10,258
7	Cleveland Indians	51.1	9,293–8,897
8	Detroit Tigers	50.7	9,235–8,979
9	Cincinnati Reds	50.6	10,457–10,211
10	Pittsburgh Pirates	50.4	10,394–10,233

SINGLE SEASON

1	Chicago Cubs	76.3	1906	116–36
2	Pittsburgh Pirates	74.1	1902	103–36
3	Chicago White Stockings	72.6	1886	90–34
4	Pittsburgh Pirates	72.4	1909	110–42
5	Cleveland Indians	72.1	1954	111–43
6	Seattle Mariners	71.6	2001	116–46
7	New York Yankees	71.4	1927	110–44
8	Detroit Wolverines	70.7	1886	87–36
9	Boston Beaneaters	70.5	1897	93–39
10	Chicago Cubs	70.4	1907	107–45

RECORD FACT

Since interleague play began in 1997, the Boston Red Sox have the best interleague winning percentage, at .605.

Win·Loss Percentage [Worst]

FRANCHISE HISTORY

1	San Diego Padres	46.2	3,611–4,201
2	Tampa Bay Rays	46.3	1,500–1,738
3	Colorado Rockies	46.9	1,871–2,117
4	Miami Marlins	47.0	1,870–2,111
	Seattle Mariners	47.0	3,062–3,455
6	Philadelphia Phillies	47.1	9,664–10,837
7	Baltimore Orioles	47.7	8,667–9,505
8	Milwaukee Brewers	47.8	3,728–4,077
9	Texas Rangers	47.9	4,355–4,733
10	New York Mets	48.0	4,285–4,647

SINGLE SEASON

1	Cleveland Spiders	13.0	1899	20–134
2	Pittsburgh Alleghenys	16.9	1890	23–113
3	Louisville Colonels	19.6	1889	27–111
4	St. Louis Browns	22.1	1897	29–102
5	Washington Nationals	23.3	1886	28–92
6	Philadelphia Athletics	23.5	1916	36–117
7	Kansas City Cowboys	24.8	1886	30–91
	Boston Braves	24.8	1935	38–115
9	New York Mets	25.0	1962	40–120
10	Washington Senators	25.2	1904	38–113

Streaks

WINS

1	New York Giants	26	1916
2	Cleveland Indians	22	2017
3	Chicago White Stockings	21	1880
	Chicago Cubs	21	1935
5	Providence Grays	20	1884
	St. Louis Maroons	20	1884
	Oakland Athletics	20	2002

LOSSES

1	Louisville Colonels	26	1889
2	Cleveland Spiders	24	1899
3	Pittsburgh Alleghenys	23	1890
	Philadelphia Phillies	23	1961
5	Philadelphia Athletics	22	1890

▲ Joe Morgan

MORGAN'S MAGIC

In 1988, the Boston Red Sox were in a rut. The team was 43–42 at the All-Star break and nine games back in the division. The decision was made to fire manager John McNamara. Less than two years earlier, he had led the team to the World Series. McNamara was replaced with Joe Morgan. Morgan was a former player who had spent most of his playing and coaching career in the minor leagues. The switch paid off. The Red Sox won 12 straight games under their new skipper, and 19 of 20. Morgan rallied the team from fourth place in the division to clinching the American League East title.

Offense By the Numbers

OFFENSE

Most runs scored in an inning	18	Chicago White Stockings	1883
Most runs scored in a game	36	Chicago Colts	1897
Most runs scored in a game	Total 49	Chicago Cubs and Philadelphia Phillies	1922
Most runs scored in a season	1,220	Boston Beaneaters	1894
Most hits in a game	33	Cleveland Indians	1932
Most hits in a season	1,783	Philadelphia Phillies	1930
Most home runs in a game	10	Toronto Blue Jays	1987
Most home runs in a season	264	Seattle Mariners	1997
Most strikeouts in a season	1,571	Milwaukee Brewers	2017
Lowest ERA in a season	2	Chicago Cubs	1907

POWER TEAM

It would be hard to argue against the 1961 New York Yankees being the greatest team of all time. The '61 Yankees dominated their division, winning 109 games in the regular season. Their pitching staff was led by Whitey Ford. He won 25 games and collected the Cy Young Award as the Yankees won their 19th World Series title. But the talk of 1961 was the home run race between Yankee teammates Roger Maris and Mickey Mantle. The two slugged home runs back and forth all summer. When the season ended, they set the record as the only two teammates to hit 50 or more home runs in the same season. Maris crushed 61 homers and Mantle knocked 54 out of the park.

▲ Mickey Mantle

Bomb Squads

SIX TEAMS THAT HAVE HIT FIVE HOME RUNS IN ONE INNING:

1	New York Giants	June 6, 1939
2	Philadelphia Phillies	June 2, 1949
3	San Francisco Giants	Aug. 23, 1961
4	Minnesota Twins	June 9, 1966
5	Milwaukee Brewers	Apr. 22, 2006
6	Washington Nationals	July 27, 2017

RECORD FACT

The Texas Rangers set a unique record in 2014 when they used 64 different players on their roster in a single season.

▲ Ed Delahanty

TWO BY TWO

Only 18 players have hit four home runs in a single game. One was unique. Ed Delahanty was a leftfielder for the Philadelphia Phillies. On July 13, 1896, Delahanty had five hits against the Chicago Colts. This included the four home runs that earned him a place in history. What makes Delahanty's feat so special is that two of his home runs were inside-the-park homers. Despite his heroics at the plate, the Phillies lost the game 9-8.

CHAPTER 4
Postseason and All-Stars

In 1908, the Chicago Cubs won the World Series, giving the team back-to-back championships. Little did they know, it would be 108 years before they earned another title. The Cubbies returned to the World Series seven times during the drought. However, they couldn't capture the crown until a historic season in 2016.

That season, Jake Arrieta led the team as its ace. He won 18 games and tossed a no-hitter on April 21, and the Cubs won 103 games during the regular season. This was their highest total since 1910.

In the World Series, the Cubs fell behind, three games to one. The curse seemed destined to continue. But the Cubs refused to give up. They rallied for three straight wins to bring a World Championship home to the Windy City. The longest championship drought in professional sports history was finally over.

POSTSEASON AND ALL-STAR RECORDS

MOST WORLD SERIES WINS (TEAM)

1	Yankees	27
2	Cardinals	11
3	Athletics	9
4	Red Sox	8
	Giants	8
6	Dodgers	6
7	Pirates	5
	Reds	5
9	Tigers	4
10	Five teams tied with 3	

MOST WORLD SERIES WINS (PLAYER)

1	Yogi Berra	10
2	Joe DiMaggio	9
3	Frankie Crosetti	8
	Bill Dickey	8
	Lou Gehrig	8
	Phil Rizzuto	8
7	Six players tied with 7	

RECORD FACT

The 2004 Red Sox are the only team in history to win a playoff series after being down 3–0. They won four straight in the American League Championship Series and went on to sweep the St. Louis Cardinals in the World Series.

RECORD FACT

All six players who won eight or more World Series rings won them as members of the New York Yankees

CAPTAIN CLUTCH

Reggie Jackson earned the nickname "Mr. October" for his ability to hit home runs in the postseason when his teams needed it most. Derek Jeter made a strong case in his playing career that he was "Mr. October 2.0." The longtime Yankees captain played in 158 postseason games in his career. That's the equivalent of almost a full regular season. His numbers speak for themselves: Jeter hit .308, collected 200 hits and 20 home runs, and drove in 61. He earned five World Series rings and was named MVP of the 2000 Series.

Jeter also made one of the greatest defensive plays in postseason history. On a base hit to right field in the seventh inning, Yankee Shane Spencer came up throwing to the plate. Unfortunately, he missed both cutoff men. Jeter sprinted across the field from his position at shortstop. He grabbed the bouncing ball and tossed a backhand flip to catcher Jorge Posada, who tagged out the runner at the plate. The acrobatic play saved a run and, for his team that was facing elimination in the game, maybe its season.

▲ **Derek Jeter**

ALL-STAR APPEARANCES

1	Hank Aaron	21
2	Willie Mays	20
	Stan Musial	20
4	Cal Ripken Jr.	19
5	Rod Carew	18
	Carl Yastrzemski	18
7	Pete Rose	17
	Ted Williams	17
9	Mickey Mantle	16
10	Five players tied with 15	

HOME RUNS

The Home Run Derby is a highlight of the All-Star Game each year. Fans fill the stadium to watch their favorite players launch home runs. In 2016, Miami Marlins slugger Giancarlo Stanton put on a show for the record books. Stanton launched 61 home runs out of Petco Park in San Diego, including two balls that traveled 497 feet (151 meters).

◀ **Giancarlo Stanton**

CHAPTER 5

The Best and the Rest

To throw a no-hitter is an incredible accomplishment for any pitcher. To throw two in a career is so rare that only 34 men have done it in the history of the game. One of them, Johnny Vander Meer, stands alone at the top of the record books. Many believe his record is the one that will never be broken. This Cincinnati Reds pitcher is the only player to ever throw back-to-back no-hitters.

Vander Meer had a losing record of 119–121 in his career. But one week in the summer of 1938 earned the switch-hitting southpaw a place in baseball immortality.

On June 11, 1938, Vander Meer took the hill against the Boston Bees and was dominant. Though he walked three batters, Vander Meer recorded 27 outs without allowing a hit. The Reds picked up the 3-0 win. But "Vandy" wasn't finished. Just four days later, he squared off against the Brooklyn Dodgers. It was the first night game in the history of legendary Ebbets Field in Brooklyn. The game was a sellout. More than 38,000 fans witnessed Vandy's second no-hitter, blanking the Dodgers 6-0. In the 80 seasons since he set the record, no one has even come close to duplicating Vander Meer's double no-no.

UNBREAKABLE RECORDS

RIPKEN'S STREAK OF CONSECUTIVE GAMES PLAYED

This book opened with a look at arguably the most unbreakable of all records for position players—**Cal Ripken Jr.'s** Iron Man streak. Ripken took the field on May 30, 1982. He was a rookie third baseman for the Baltimore Orioles. That was the first of 2,632 consecutive games Ripken started, shattering **Lou Gehrig's** mark of 2,130 games.

Why the record won't be broken: Ripken played through a twisted knee, multiple ankle injuries, and even a broken nose without missing a start. Today, players routinely get "rest days." A team may be paying a player $20 million per season. In that case, they are more likely to rest a player with an injury rather than allowing them to play through it, risking their investment.

▲ Cal Ripken Jr.

▲ Joe DiMaggio

DIMAGGIO'S HITTING STREAK

For two months in the summer of 1941, **Joe DiMaggio**, the "Yankee Clipper," crafted a record that has stood unthreatened for more than 75 years. DiMaggio, the Hall of Fame centerfielder for the New York Yankees, hit safely in 56 consecutive games. The streak was so impressive at the time, DiMaggio beat out Red Sox leftfielder **Ted Williams** for the MVP Award, despite Williams batting .406 for the season.

Why the record won't be broken: In DiMaggio's era, pitchers regularly pitched complete games. By the third or fourth at bat, a hitter had a good read on the pitcher and was often more successful. Today, teams use specialists to relieve starting pitchers. This means that a batter can face potentially three or more pitchers in a full game, facing well-rested pitchers late in the game. The closest any player has come was **Pete Rose**. He built a 44-game hitting streak in 1978. Since then, no one has come seriously close to Joltin' Joe's record.

CY YOUNG'S WIN TOTAL

Cy Young was so dominant during his 22-year Hall of Fame career, they named the annual award for the best pitcher in each league after him. Young led the league in ERA twice, complete games three times, and even strikeouts twice. But it is his 511 wins that are a lock to be an unbeatable record. In the last 50 years, the closest any pitcher has come to Young's 511 wins was **Greg Maddux**. He notched 355 victories and pitched for 23 seasons. Yet he still came up 157 wins short of breaking Young's record.

Why the record won't be broken: Pitchers today don't get anywhere near as many starts as Young did. In today's five-man rotations, a pitcher might get 35 starts in a season if he stays healthy. Young had 11 seasons with more than 40 starts, including seasons when he started 46, 47, and 49 games. He had five seasons with 30-plus wins. Maddux reached 20 wins only twice in his career. The increased use of relievers also cuts down on wins, as a struggling pitcher may not have the chance to battle back in a game. Fewer annual starts, fewer complete games, and shorter average careers means this record is in no danger of being broken.

▲ Cy Young

▼ Nolan Ryan

NOLAN RYAN'S STRIKEOUTS

Nolan Ryan is known for his seven no-hitters—a record unlikely to ever be broken. But his 5,714 strikeouts are an equally impressive accomplishment. Ryan built a career as a pure fastball pitcher who wasn't afraid to pitch inside on batters. He led the league in strikeouts 11 times in his career, including four times after he turned 40.

Why the record won't be broken: Few players in MLB history have endured for as many seasons and Ryan did. Current superstar and Dodgers ace **Clayton Kershaw**, for example, is on pace with Ryan for strikeouts per start over the course of his career. Ryan averaged 7.39 K's per start for his career. Kershaw is at 7.29. But the reality is, Kershaw has struggled to stay healthy and is unlikely to match Ryan's 27 seasons on the mound. To take the K crown from Ryan, a pitcher would need to average more than 285 strikeouts every year for 20 seasons.

▲ Clayton Kershaw

THE 40/40 CLUB

Traditionally, base stealers are lean, lanky players with bodies built for speed, not power. Likewise, power hitters have rarely been known for being fleet of foot. That's what makes the feat of hitting 40 home runs and swiping 40 bases in the same season so impressive. Only four players have accomplished the 40/40 season: **Jose Canseco** in 1988, **Barry Bonds** in 1996, **Alex Rodriguez** in 1998, and **Alfonso Soriano** in 2006.

▲ Jose Canseco

▲ Kendrys Morales

HOMERS FROM BOTH SIDES OF THE PLATE IN THE SAME INNING

Hitting a home run is hard. Hitting two in a game is really hard. Hitting two in the same inning is rare. But hitting two in the same inning, one from each side of the plate, has only happened three times. On April 8, 1993, Indians infielder **Carlos Baerga** was the first to accomplish this rare feat. **Mark Bellhorn** was next, knocking two out on August 29, 2002, as a member of the Chicago Cubs. **Kendrys Morales** was the last player to homer from both sides of the plate in the same inning. His big day came July 30, 2012, against the Texas Rangers.

▲ **Justin Verlander**

THE PITCHERS' TRIPLE CROWN

Pitchers have their own triple crown that recognizes leading the league in wins, strikeouts, and earned run average for the season. Though not as rare as the batting triple crown, no pitcher has earned a triple crown since 2011. That year, each league produced a triple crown winner. In the American League, Tigers pitcher **Justin Verlander** went 24–5, with an ERA of 2.40 and 250 strikeouts. In the National League, Dodgers ace **Clayton Kershaw** tallied a record of 21–5 with a 2.28 ERA and 248 strikeouts to sweep the big three.

UNASSISTED TRIPLE PLAY

The double play is often called "a pitcher's best friend." For eight pitchers in history, their best friend was an unassisted triple play. Pulling off the unassisted triple play requires a lot of elements that are out of a player's control. First, there must be no outs. Next, there must be at least two men on base. Finally, in all eight cases, a line drive was hit sharply right at a fielder. It is usually hit up the middle with baserunners on the move. The ball is caught and the fielder can step on second base and tag the runner coming from first base. Though they are rare, they are actually very easy to execute for the fielder. It is all about being in the right place at the right time.

▲ **Jonathan Schoop**

Gold Glove Leaders

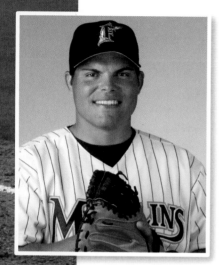

▲ Ivan Rodriguez

CATCHER

1	Ivan Rodriguez	13
2	Johnny Bench	10
3	Yadier Molina	8*
4	Bob Boone	7
5	Jim Sundberg	6
6	Bill Freehan	5
7	Del Crandall	4
	Charles Johnson	4
	Mike Matheny	4
	Tony Pena	4
	Salvador Perez	4*

PITCHER

1	Greg Maddux	18
2	Jim Kaat	16
3	Bob Gibson	9
4	Bobby Shantz	8
5	Mark Langston	7
	Mike Mussina	7
7	Ron Guidry	5
	Phil Niekro	5
	Kenny Rogers	5
10	Mark Buehrle	4
	Zack Greinke	4*
	Jim Palmer	4

active player

FIRST BASE

1	Keith Hernandez	11
2	Don Mattingly	9
3	George Scott	8
4	Vic Power	7
	Bill White	7
6	Wes Parker	6
	J.T. Snow	6
8	Mark Teixeira	5
9	Steve Garvey	4
	Adrian Gonzalez	4
	Mark Grace	4
	Eric Hosmer	4*

SECOND BASE

1	Roberto Alomar	10
2	Ryne Sandberg	9
3	Bill Mazeroski	8
	Frank White	8
5	Joe Morgan	5
	Bobby Richardson	5
7	Craig Biggio	4
	Bret Boone	4
	Bobby Grich	4
	Orlando Hudson	4
	Dustin Pedroia	4*
	Brandon Phillips*	4

▲ Ryne Sandberg

active player

49

Gold Glove Leaders

▲ Ozzie Smith

SHORTSTOP

1	Ozzie Smith	13
2	Omar Vizquel	11
3	Luis Aparicio	9
4	Mark Belanger	8
5	Dave Concepcion	5
	Derek Jeter	5
7	Tony Fernandez	4
	Jimmy Rollins	4
	Alan Trammell	4
10	Brandon Crawford	3*
	J.J. Hardy	3
	Barry Larkin	3
	Roy McMillan	3
	Rey Ordonez	3
	Andrelton Simmons	3*

active player

RECORD FACT

Ozzie Smith's 13 Gold Glove Awards were for 13 consecutive seasons, from 1980 through 1992. Smith also won the National League's Silver Slugger Award in 1987.

THIRD BASE

1	Brooks Robinson	16
2	Mike Schmidt	10
3	Scott Rolen	8
4	Buddy Bell	6
	Eric Chavez	6
	Robin Ventura	6
7	Nolan Arenado*	5
	Adrian Beltre	5*
	Ken Boyer	5
	Doug Rader	5
	Ron Santo	5

RECORD FACT

Orioles third baseman Brooks Robinson won the Rawlings Gold Glove Award 16 seasons in a row from 1960 to 1975.

OUTFIELD

1	Roberto Clemente	12
	Willie Mays	12
3	Ken Griffey Jr.	10
	Andruw Jones	10
	Al Kaline	10
	Ichiro Suzuki	10*
7	Torii Hunter	9
8	Paul Blair	8
	Barry Bonds	8
	Andre Dawson	8
	Jim Edmonds	8
	Dwight Evans	8
	Garry Maddox	8

active player

▲ Ken Griffey Jr.

Most Seasons Played

CAREER

1	**Cap Anson**	27	Forest Citys/Athletics/White Stockings/Colts	1871–1897
	Nolan Ryan	27	Mets/Angels/Astros/Rangers	1966, 1968–1993
3	**Deacon McGuire**	26	Blue Stockings/Wolverines/Quakers/Blues/Broncos/Statesmen/Senators/Superbas/Tigers/Highlanders/Americans/Red Sox/Naps	1884–1888, 1890–1908, 1910, 1912
	Tommy John	26	Indians/White Sox/Dodgers/Yankees/Angels/Athletics	1963–1974, 1976–1989
5	**Bobby Wallace**	25	Spiders/Perfectos/Cardinals/Browns	1894–1918
	Eddie Collins	25	Athletics/White Sox	1906–1930
	Jim Kaat	25	Senators/Twins/White Sox/Phillies/Yankees/Cardinals	1959–1983
	Charlie Hough	25	Dodgers/Rangers/White Sox/Marlins	1970–1994
	Rickey Henderson	25	Athletics/Yankees/Blue Jays/Padres/Angels/Mets/Mariners/Red Sox/Dodgers	1979–2003
	Jamie Moyer	25	Cubs/Rangers/Cardinals/Orioles/Red Sox/Mariners/Phillies/Rockies	1986–1991, 1993–2010, 2012

RECORD FACT

The oldest player to hit a home run in a major league game was Julio Franco, who was 48 when he went deep for the Mets in 2007. The youngest ever was Tommy Brown, who was just 17 years old when he hit his first round-tripper for the Brooklyn Dodgers in 1945.

▲ Cap Anson

FIVE-DECADE PHENOMS?

Some records are more controversial than others. Pitcher Nick Altrock and outfielder/third baseman Minnie Minoso share the record as the only two players to appear in a game in five different decades. Both records are considered "gimmicks" by many baseball historians. Altrock set the record by appearing in a single game in 1933 at the age of 56 with the Washington Senators. Minoso took a similar path to the record books. He returned to the Chicago White Sox in 1980, appearing in two games at the age of 54 and going 0-2 at the plate.

▲ Nick Altrock

THE RYAN EXPRESS

Altrock's and Minoso's final appearances might have been gimmicks, but Nolan Ryan was the real deal. The Hall of Fame pitcher played until he was almost 47 years old. Ryan had the numbers to back up his age. In 1987, he posted a league-leading 2.76 earned run average at the age of 40. Ryan went on to win 71 games and strike out more than 1,400 hitters after he turned 40 years old. He was so dominant in his 40s, Ryan led the league in strikeouts every season from 1987 through 1990.

▲ Nolan Ryan

Wins By a Manager

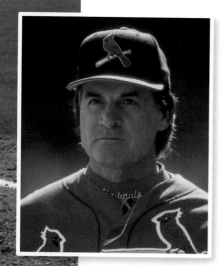

▲ Tony LaRussa

CAREER

1	Connie Mack	3,731	Pirates/Athletics	1894–1896, 1901–1950
2	John McGraw	2,763	Orioles/Giants	1899, 1901–1932
3	Tony LaRussa	2,728	White Sox/Athletics/ Cardinals	1979–2011
4	Bobby Cox	2,504	Blue Jays/Braves	1978–1985, 1990–2010
5	Joe Torre	2,326	Mets/Braves/Cardinals/ Yankees/Dodgers	1977–1984, 1990–2010
6	Sparky Anderson	2,194	Reds/Tigers	1970–1995
7	Bucky Harris	2,158	Senators/Tigers/Red Sox/Phillies/Yankees	1924–1943, 1947–1948, 1950–1956
8	Joe McCarthy	2,125	Cubs/Yankees/Red Sox	1926–1946, 1948–1950
9	Walter Alston	2,040	Dodgers	1954–1976
10	Leo Durocher	2,008	Dodgers/Giants/ Cubs/Astros	1939–1946, 1948–1955, 1966–1973

DOUBLE DUTY

It might sound crazy today, but more than 200 major leaguers have managed a team while they were a player. It was common in the early days of baseball for a team to name one of its players to lead the squad. Legendary players including Ty Cobb, Rogers Hornsby, and Cy Young, all took a turn at managing the teams they played on. The last man to wear both hats was Pete Rose. He managed and played for the Cincinnati Reds from 1984 through 1986.

World Series Wins By a Manager

CAREER

1	**Joe McCarthy**	7	Cubs/Yankees/Red Sox	1926–1946, 1948–1950
	Casey Stengel	7	Dodgers/Bees/Braves/ Yankees/Mets	1934–1936, 1938–1943, 1949–1960, 1962–1965
3	**Connie Mack**	5	Pirates/Athletics	1894–1896, 1901–1950
4	**Walter Alston**	4	Dodgers	1954–1976
	Joe Torre	4	Mets/Braves/Cardinals/ Yankees/Dodgers	1977–1984, 1990–2010
6	**John McGraw**	3	Orioles/Giants	1899, 1901–1932
	Miller Huggins	3	Cardinals/Yankees	1913–1929
	Sparky Anderson	3	Reds/Tigers	1970–1995
	Tony LaRussa	3	White Sox/Athletics/Cardinals	1979–2011
	Bruce Bochy	3	Padres/Giants	1995–2017*

*active player

▲ **Connie Mack**

RECORD FACT

Former Braves skipper Bobby Cox was ejected 161 times during his career, including twice in the World Series.

It isn't always a good thing to be a record holder. Just ask these players who made the list of the "best of the worst."

Strikeouts

▲ Jim Thome

CAREER

1	Reggie Jackson	2,597	Athletics/Orioles/Yankees/Angels	1967–1987
2	Jim Thome	2,548	Indians/Phillies/White Sox/Dodgers/Twins/Orioles	1991–2012
3	Adam Dunne	2,379	Reds/Diamondbacks/Nationals/White Sox/Athletics	2001–2014
4	Sammy Sosa	2,306	Rangers/White Sox/Cubs/Orioles	1989–2005, 2007
5	Alex Rodriguez	2,287	Mariners/Rangers/Yankees	1994–2013, 2015–2016
6	Andres Galarraga	2,003	Expos/Cardinals/Rockies/Braves/Rangers/Giants/Angels	1985–1998, 2000–2004
7	Jose Canseco	1,942	Athletics/Rangers/Red Sox/Blue Jays/Devil Rays/Yankees/White Sox	1985–2001
8	Willie Stargell	1,936	Pirates	1962–1982
9	Mike Cameron	1,901	White Sox/Reds/Mariners/Mets/Padres/Brewers/Red Sox/Marlins	1995–2011
10	Mike Schmidt	1,883	Phillies	1972–1989

RECORD FACT

Sandy Koufax is a Hall of Fame pitcher and a Hall of Shame hitter. Koufax had 12 plate appearances in 1955 and struck out 12 straight times.

SINGLE SEASON

1	Mark Reynolds	223	Diamondbacks	2009*
2	Adam Dunn	222	White Sox	2012
3	Chris Davis	219	Orioles	2016*
4	Chris Carter	212	Astros	2013*
5	Mark Reynolds	211	Diamondbacks	2010*
6	Chris Davis	208	Orioles	2015*
	Aaron Judge	208	Yankees	2017*
8	Chris Carter	206	Brewers	2016*
9	Drew Stubbs	205	Reds	2011
10	Mark Reynolds	204	Diamondbacks	2008*

active player

▲ Mark Reynolds

AARON JUDGE

In 2017, Yankees rookie rightfielder Aaron Judge had one of the greatest rookie campaigns in modern times. The young slugger led the American League in home runs, crushing 52, and runs scored, with 128. Judge also showed patience at the plate, leading the league in walks. But he is also remembered for a more dubious record. Judge struck out a league-leading 208 times in 2017. That ranks sixth all-time for most K's in a season.

◀ Aaron Judge

▲ Bill Dahlen

WINLESS CAREERS

Cy Young notched 511 wins as a major league pitcher. Juan Alvarez and Ed Olwine would have settled for just one. The two pitchers share the record for most games pitched without earning a single win. Alvarez appeared in 80 games during his four-year career, posting a record of 0–5. Olwine made 80 relief appearances for the Atlanta Braves. He ended his three-year career with a record of 0–1.

Errors

CAREER

1	**Herman Long**	1,096	Cowboys/Beaneaters/Highlanders/Tigers/Phillies	1889–1904
2	**Bill Dahlen**	1,080	Colts/Orphans/Superbas/Giants/Doves/Dodgers	1891–1911
3	**Deacon White**	1,018	Forest Citys/Red Stockings/White Stockings/Reds/Bisons/Wolverines/Alleghenys	1871–1890
4	**Germany Smith**	1,009	Mountain City/Blues/Grays/Reds/Bridegrooms/Browns	1884–1898
5	**Tommy Corcoran**	996	Burghers/Athletics/Grooms/Bridegrooms/Reds/Giants	1890–1907
6	**Fred Pfeffer**	980	Trojans/White Stockings/Pirates/Colonels/Giants/Colts	1882–1897
7	**Cap Anson**	976	Forest Citys/Athletics/White Stockings/Colts	1871–1897
8	**John Ward**	952	Grays/Gothams/Giants/Ward's Wonders/Grooms	1878–1894
9	**Jack Glasscock**	895	Blues/Outlaw Reds/Maroons/Hoosiers/Giants/Browns/Pirates/Colonels/Senators	1879–1895
10	**Ed McKean**	892	Blues/Spiders/Perfectos	1887–1899

Hit Batsmen

CAREER

#	Name			
1	Gus Weyhing	277	Athletics/Ward's Wonders/Phillies/ Pirates/Colonels/ Senators/Cardinals/ Superbas/Reds/Blues	1887–1896, 1898–1901
2	Chick Fraser	219	Colonels/Spiders/ Phillies/Athletics/ Beaneaters/Reds/Cubs	1896–1909
3	Pink Hawley	210	Browns/Pirates/Reds/ Giants/Brewers	1892–1901
4	Walter Johnson	205	Senators	1907–1927
5	Eddie Plank	190	Athletics/Terriers/Browns	1901–1917
	Randy Johnson	190	Expos/Mariners/ Astros/Diamondbacks/ Yankees/Giants	1988–2009
7	Tim Wakefield	186	Pirates/Red Sox	1992–1993, 1995–2011
8	Tony Mullane	185	Wolverines/Eclipse/ Browns/Blue Stockings/ Red Stockings/Reds/ Orioles/Spiders	1880–1884, 1886–1894
9	Joe McGinnity	179	Orioles/Superbas/Giants	1899–1908
10	Charlie Hough	174	Dodgers/Rangers/ White Sox/Marlins	1970–1994

▲ Randy Johnson

HIT BY HOWARD

Hitters might have been careful not to dig in too tight in the batter's box against pitcher Howard Ehmke. From 1920 to 1927, Ehmke led the American League in hit batsmen six times. Despite his wildness, Ehmke won 166 games over a 15-year career. This included a 20-win season for the Boston Red Sox in 1923.

Wild Pitches

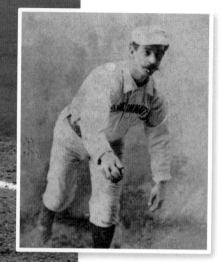

▲ Tony Mullane

CAREER

1	**Tony Mullane**	343	Wolverines/Eclipse/ Browns/BlueStockings/ Red Stockings/Reds/ Orioles/Spiders	1881–1884, 1886–1894
2	**Nolan Ryan**	277	Mets/Angels/ Astros/Rangers	1966, 1968–1993
3	**Mickey Welch**	274	Trojans/Gothams/Giants	1880–1892
4	**Bobby Mathews**	253	Kekiongas/Canaries/ Mutuals/Reds/Grays/ Red Stockings/Athletics	1871–1877, 1879, 1881–1887
5	**Tim Keefe**	240	Trojans/Metropolitans/ Giants/Phillies	1880–1893
	Gus Weyhing	240	Athletics/Ward's Wonders/ Phillies/Pirates/Colonels/ Senators/Cardinals/ Superbas/Reds/Blues	1887–1896, 1898–1901
7	**Phil Niekro**	226	Braves/Yankees/ Indians/Blue Jays	1964–1987
8	**Pud Galvin**	221	Brown Stockings/Bisons/ Alleghenys/Burghers/ Pirates/Browns	1875, 1879–1892
	Will White	221	Red Stockings/ Reds/Wolverines	1877–1886
	Mark Baldwin	221	White Stockings/ Solons/Pirates/Giants	1887–1893

SINGLE SEASON

1	Mark Baldwin	83	Solons	1889
2	Tony Mullane	63	Blue Stockings	1884
	Bill Stemmyer	63	Beaneaters	1886
4	Mike Morrison	62	Blues	1887
5	Matt Kilroy	61	Orioles	1886
6	Ed Seward	58	Athletics	1887
7	Jersey Bakley	56	Keystones/Quicksteps/Cowboys	1884
	Gus Weyhing	56	Athletics	1888
9	Ed Seward	54	Athletics	1888
10	Tony Mullane	53	Red Stockings	1886

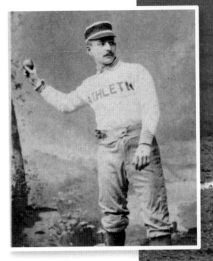

▲ Ed Seward

▲ Rick Ankiel

WILD THING

In the third inning of the 2000 National League Division Series, Cardinals pitcher Rick Ankiel threw five wild pitches. This was the most wild pitches ever thrown in a postseason inning. Ankiel went on to throw four more wild pitches in the NLCS. He never recovered from his wildness, and his pitching career came to an early end. Ankiel reinvented himself as an outfielder and went on to hit home runs for six different teams.

Read More

Braun, Eric. *Baseball Stats and the Stories Behind Them: What Every Fan Needs to Know.* Sports Stats and Stories. North Mankato, Minn.: Capstone Press, 2016.

Morey, Allan. *Baseball Records.* Minneapolis, Minn.: Bellwether Media, Inc., 2018.

Editors of Sports Illustrated Kids. *Baseball: Then to WOW!* Sports Illustrated Kids Then to WOW! New York: Time, Inc., 2016.

Internet Sites

Use FactHound to find Internet sites related to this book.

Visit *www.facthound.com*

Just type in 9781543554632 and go.

Super-cool stuff! Check out projects, games and lots more at
www.capstonekids.com

Index

Aaron, Hank, 5, 7, 11, 12, 14, 41
Alexander, Grover, 23, 25, 28
Alomar, Roberto, 49
Altrock, Nick, 53
Altuve, Jose, 6
Ankiel, Rick, 61
Anson, Cap, 11, 12, 14, 16, 52, 58
Aparicio, Luis, 50
Arenado, Nolan, 51
Arrieta, Jake, 38
Atlanta Braves, 7, 9, 10, 11, 12, 14,
    18, 20, 23, 24, 25, 26, 28, 31,
    34, 54, 55, 56, 58, 60

Baerga, Carlos, 46
Bakley, Jersey, 61
Baldwin, Mark, 60, 61
Baltimore Orioles, 5, 7, 8, 9, 10, 11,
    13, 16, 18, 19, 20, 21, 23, 24,
    31, 34, 43, 51, 52, 54, 55, 56,
    57, 59, 60, 61
Banks, Ernie, 8
Barnes, Ross, 10
Barria, Jaime, 21
Baylor, Don, 21
Beckley, Jake, 9, 18
Belanger, Mark, 50
Bell, Buddy, 51
Bellhorn, Mark, 46
Beltre, Adrian, 51
Bench, Johnny, 48
Berra, Yogi, 39
Biggio, Craig, 17, 21, 49
Blair, Paul, 51
Blyleven, Bert, 24, 28, 30
Boggs, Wade, 16
Bonds, Barry, 5, 7, 11, 12, 20,
    46, 51
Bond, Tommy, 26
Boone, Bob, 48
Boone, Bret, 49
Boston Red Sox, 6, 7, 8, 9, 10, 11,
    12, 14, 16, 17, 18, 19, 20, 21,
    23, 24, 25, 26, 27, 28, 29, 31,
    32, 33, 35, 39, 43, 52, 54, 55,
    56, 59
Bottomley, Jim, 13
Boyer, Ken, 51
Bradley, George, 28
Brett, George, 17
Brock, Lou, 19

Brouthers, Dan, 10, 18
Brown, Mordecai, 26, 27
Brown, Tom, 11
Buehrle, Mark, 48
Buffington, Charlie, 24
Buffinton, Charlie, 23
Burkett, Jesse, 9, 16
Burns, George, 17

Cabrera, Miguel, 6
Canseco, Jose, 46, 56
Carew, Rod, 16, 41
Carey, Max, 19
Carlton, Steve, 24, 25, 30
Carter, Chris, 57
Chavez, Eric, 51
Chiacgo Cubs, 7, 8, 9, 10, 12, 17,
    19, 20, 21, 23, 24, 25, 26, 27,
    28, 31, 32, 33, 35, 36, 38, 46,
    52, 54, 55, 56, 59
Chicago Cubs, 7, 8, 9, 10, 12, 17,
    19, 20, 21, 23, 24, 25, 26, 27,
    28, 31, 32, 33, 35, 36, 38, 46,
    52, 54, 55, 56, 59
Chicago White Sox, 7, 8, 9, 10, 16,
    19, 20, 21, 24, 25, 26, 28, 29,
    31, 52, 53, 54, 55, 56, 57, 59
Cincinnati Reds, 7, 9, 10, 11, 14,
    16, 17, 18, 19, 20, 21, 23, 24,
    25, 26, 28, 30, 31, 33, 39, 42,
    54, 55, 56, 57, 58, 59, 60
Clarke, Fred, 18
Clarkson, John, 23, 25
Clemens, Roger, 23, 24, 30
Clemente, Roberto, 51
Cleveland Indians, 7, 8, 9, 10,
    14, 16, 17, 18, 20, 21, 24, 25,
    26, 28, 31, 33, 35, 36, 46, 52,
    56, 60
Cobb, Ty, 9, 10, 11, 12, 14, 15, 16,
    17, 18, 19, 54
Coleman, Vince, 19
Collins, Eddie, 16, 19, 52
Colorado Rockies, 17, 22, 34, 52, 56
Comiskey, Charlie, 19
Concepcion, Dave, 50
Connor, Roger, 18
Coombs, Jack, 28, 29
Corcoran, Tommy, 58
Crandall, Del, 48
Crawford, Brandon, 50
Crawford, Sam, 9, 18
Crosetti, Frankie, 39

Dahlen, Bill, 58
Daily, Hugh, 24
Daubert, Jake, 9
Davis, Chris, 57
Davis, George, 18

Davis, Harry, 18
Dawson, Andre, 51
Delahanty, Ed, 10, 37
Delgado, Carlos, 17
Detroit Tigers, 6, 9, 10, 11, 12, 14,
    15, 16, 17, 18, 19, 21, 31, 33,
    39, 47, 52, 54, 55, 58
Devlin, Jim, 25, 26
Dickey, Bill, 39
DiMaggio, Joe, 32, 39, 43
Driscoll, Denny, 27
Drysdale, Don, 29
Duffy, Hugh, 10
Dunn, Adam, 57
Dunne, Adam, 56

Eckersley, Dennis, 31
Edmonds, Jim, 51
Evans, Dwight, 51

Fernandez, Tony, 50
Ford, Whitey, 36
Foxx, Jimmie, 8, 12
Franco, John, 31
Franco, Julio, 52
Fraser, Chick, 59
Freehan, Bill, 48

Gagne, Eric, 31
Galarraga, Andres, 56
Galvin, Pud, 23, 25, 28, 60
Garvey, Steve, 49
Gehrig, Lou, 5, 8, 11, 12, 32, 39, 43
Gehringer, Charlie, 17
Gentile, Jim, 8
Gibson, Bob, 27, 28, 29, 48
Glasscock, Jack, 58
Gonzalez, Adrian, 49
Grace, Mark, 49
Greenberg, Hank, 12, 17
Greinke, Zack, 29, 48
Grich, Bobby, 49
Griffey Jr., Ken, 7, 51
Guidry, Ron, 48

Hafner, Travis, 8
Halladay, Roy, 27
Hamilton, Billy, 10, 11, 19
Hardy, J.J., 50
Harper, Bryce, 20
Hawley, Pink, 59
Hecker, Guy, 23, 24, 25
Helton, Todd, 17
Henderson, Rickey, 11, 19, 20, 52
Herman, Billy, 17
Hernandez, Keith, 49
Hershiser, Orel, 28, 29
Hoffman, Trevor, 31
Hornsby, Rogers, 9, 10, 15, 54

Hosmer, Eric, 49
Hough, Charlie, 52, 59
Hubbell, Carl, 29
Hudson, Orlando, 49
Hunter, Torii, 51
Hunt, Ron, 21
Hutchinson, Bill, 25

Jackson, Joe, 10
Jackson, Reggie, 40, 56
Jennings, Hughie, 21
Jeter, Derek, 14, 16, 40, 50
Johnson, Charles, 48
Johnson, Randy, 24, 30, 59
Johnson, Walter, 23, 24, 25, 27,
    28, 29, 59
John, Tommy, 52
Jones, Andruw, 51
Joss, Addie, 26, 27
Judge, Aaron, 57

Kaat, Jim, 48, 52
Kaline, Al, 51
Keefe, Tim, 23, 27, 60
Keeler, Willie, 9, 10, 11, 16
Keller, Willie, 16
Kelley, Joe, 11, 18
Kendall, Jason, 21
Kershaw, Clayton, 22, 30, 45, 47
Kilroy, Matt, 23, 24, 61
Klein, Chuck, 12, 15, 17
Koufax, Sandy, 24, 30, 56
Lajoie, Nap, 10, 17

Langston, Mark, 48
Larkin, Barry, 50
Larsen, Don, 26
Latham, Arlie, 11, 19
Lazzeri, Tony, 13
Leach, Tommy, 9
Lee, Carlos, 8
Leonard, Dutch, 27
Long, Herman, 58
Los Angeles Angels, 7, 8, 11, 12,
    13, 16, 19, 20, 21, 24, 25, 28,
    31, 52, 56, 60
Los Angeles Dodgers, 7, 8, 9, 10,
    11, 18, 19, 20, 21, 22, 23, 24,
    25, 26, 28, 29, 31, 33, 39, 42,
    45, 47, 52, 54, 55, 56, 58, 59
Lundgren, Carl, 27

Maddox, Garry, 51
Maddux, Greg, 23, 24, 30, 44, 48
Maglie, Sal, 29
Mantle, Mickey, 20, 32, 36, 41
Maris, Roger, 7, 32, 36
Martinez, Pedro, 30
Matheny, Mike, 48

Mathews, Bobby, 60
Mathewson, Christy, 23, 26, 27, 28
Mattingly, Don, 8, 49
Mays, Willie, 7, 11, 41, 51
Mazeroski, Bill, 49
McCormick, Jim, 25
McCovey, Willie, 8
McGann, Dan, 21
McGinnity, Joe, 59
McGuire, Deacon, 52
McGwire, Mark, 7, 20
McKean, Ed, 58
McMillan, Roy, 50
Medwick, Joe, 17
Miami Marlins, 6, 7, 8, 16, 19, 31, 34, 41, 52, 56, 59
Milne, Pete, 8
Milwaukee Brewers, 7, 8, 11, 12, 14, 21, 24, 25, 28, 31, 34, 36, 37, 56, 57, 59
Minnesota Twins, 7, 14, 16, 17, 20, 21, 24, 25, 28, 30, 31, 37, 52, 56
Minoso, Minnie, 21, 53
Molina, Yadier, 48
Molitor, Paul, 14
Morales, Kendrys, 46
Morgan, Joe, 20, 35, 49
Morris, Ed, 28
Morrison, Mike, 61
Moyer, Jamie, 30, 52
Mullane, Tony, 59, 60, 61
Murray, Eddie, 8
Musial, Stan, 11, 12, 14, 17, 41
Mussina, Mike, 48
Myers, Randy, 31

Nathan, Joe, 31
New York Mets, 7, 8, 11, 19, 20, 21, 23, 24, 25, 28, 29, 31, 34, 52, 54, 55, 56, 60
New York Yankees, 7, 8, 10, 11, 12, 13, 14, 16, 18, 19, 20, 21, 23, 24, 25, 26, 31, 32, 33, 36, 39, 40, 43, 52, 54, 55, 56, 57, 59, 60
Nichols, Kid, 23
Nicol, Hugh, 19
Niekro, Phil, 25, 48, 60
Nuxhall, Joe, 30

Oakland Athletics, 8, 9, 10, 11, 12, 14, 15, 16, 17, 18, 19, 20, 21, 24, 25, 28, 29, 31, 34, 35, 39, 52, 54, 55, 56, 58, 59, 60, 61
O'Doul, Lefty, 10, 15
O'Neill, Tip, 10, 11
Ordonez, Rey, 50

Orr, Dave, 18
Ortiz, David, 17
Ott, Mel, 20

Palmer, Jim, 30, 48
Papelbon, Jonathan, 31
Parker, Wes, 49
Pedroia, Dustin, 49
Pena, Tony, 48
Perez, Salvador, 48
Perry, Gaylord, 24, 25
Pfeffer, Fred, 58
Pfiester, Jack, 26, 27
Philadelphia Phillies, 7, 8, 10, 11, 12, 14, 15, 16, 17, 18, 19, 20, 21, 23, 24, 25, 27, 28, 31, 34, 35, 36, 37, 52, 54, 56, 58, 59, 60
Phillips, Brandon, 49
Pittsburg Pirates, 7, 9, 11, 12, 14, 16, 17, 18, 19, 20, 21, 23, 24, 25, 26, 28, 33, 39, 54, 55, 56, 58, 59, 60
Plank, Eddie, 28, 59
Power, Vic, 49
Pujols, Albert, 7, 8, 12

Radbourn, Charles "Old Hoss", 23, 24, 25
Rader, Doug, 51
Raines, Tim, 19
Ramirez, Manny, 8
Ramsey, Toad, 24
Reardon, Jeff, 31
Reitz, Heinie, 18
Reynolds, Mark, 57
Richardson, Bobby, 49
Ripken Jr., Cal, 5, 41, 43
Rivera, Mariano, 31
Rizzuto, Phil, 39
Robinson, Brooks, 51
Robinson, Frank, 7, 21
Robinson, Wilbert, 13
Rodriguez, Alex, 7, 8, 11, 12, 46, 56
Rodriguez, Francisco, 31
Rodriguez, Ivan, 48
Rogers, Kenny, 48
Rolen, Scott, 51
Rollins, Jimmy, 50
Rose, Pete, 11, 14, 16, 17, 41, 43, 54
Roush, Edd, 9
Ruth, Babe, 7, 10, 11, 12, 20, 32
Ryan, Nolan, 24, 25, 28, 45, 52, 53, 60

Sandberg, Ryne, 49

San Diego Padres, 8, 11, 14, 19, 20, 23, 24, 25, 31, 34, 52, 55, 56
San Francisco Giants, 7, 8, 9, 10, 11, 12, 13, 15, 16, 18, 19, 20, 21, 23, 24, 25, 26, 27, 28, 29, 31, 33, 35, 37, 39, 54, 55, 56, 58, 59, 60
Santo, Ron, 51
Schmidt, Mike, 51, 56
Schoop, Jonathan, 47
Scott, George, 49
Seattle Mariners, 7, 8, 11, 12, 15, 16, 19, 20, 24, 25, 33, 34, 36, 52, 56, 59
Seaver, Tom, 24, 28, 30
Seward, Ed, 61
Sexson, Richie, 8
Shantz, Bobby, 48
Shaw, Dupee, 24
Show, Eric, 14
Simmons, Al, 15
Simmons, Andrelton, 50
Sisler, George, 10, 15
Smith, Germany, 58
Smith, Lee, 31
Smith, Ozzie, 50
Smoltz, John, 31
Snow, J.T., 49
Soriano, Alfonso, 46
Sosa, Sammy, 7, 56
Spahn, Warren, 23, 25, 28
Spalding, Al, 26
Spaulding, Al, 23
Speaker, Tris, 9, 10, 14, 16, 17, 18
Stanton, Giancarlo, 6, 7, 41
Stemmyer, Bill, 61
St. Louis Cardinals, 7, 8, 9, 10, 11, 12, 13, 14, 15, 17, 18, 19, 20, 21, 23, 24, 25, 26, 27, 28, 29, 31, 32, 33, 39, 52, 54, 55, 56, 59, 60, 61
Stubbs, Drew, 57
Sundberg, Jim, 48
Sutton, Don, 24, 25, 28
Suzuki, Ichiro, 9, 15, 16, 51
Sweeney, Bill, 24

Tamp Bay Rays, 8, 34, 56
Teixeira, Mark, 49
Terry, Bill, 15
Texas Rangers, 5, 7, 8, 11, 12, 24, 25, 28, 31, 34, 37, 46, 52, 56, 59, 60
Thigpen, Bobby, 31
Thomas, Frank, 20
Thome, Jim, 7, 20, 56
Thompson, Sam, 10, 18

Toronto Blue Jays, 5, 11, 14, 17, 19, 20, 23, 24, 25, 36, 52, 54, 56, 60
Trammell, Alan, 50
Trout, Mike, 13
Tucker, Tommy, 21
Turner, Tuck, 10

Utley, Chase, 21

Vander Meer, Johnny, 42
Ventura, Robin, 8, 51
Verlander, Justin, 47
Vizquel, Omar, 50

Wagner, Billy, 31
Wagner, Honus, 9, 14, 16, 17, 18, 19
Wakefield, Tim, 59
Wallace, Bobby, 52
Walsh, Ed, 26
Waner, Lloyd, 16
Waner, Paul, 17, 18
Ward, John, 19, 23, 26, 58
Webb, Earl, 17
Weintraub, Phil, 13
Welch, Mickey, 60
Werden, Perry, 18
Weyhing, Gus, 59, 60, 61
White, Bill, 49
White, Deacon, 58
White, Doc, 29
White, Frank, 49
Whiten, Mark, 13
White, Will, 25, 60
Williams, Jimmy, 18
Williams, Ted, 8, 10, 20, 41, 43
Wilson, Chief, 18
Wilson, Hack, 12
Wood, Joe, 26

Yastrzemski, Carl, 6, 14, 17, 20, 41
Yost, Eddie, 20
Young, Anthony, 29
Young, Cy, 23, 25, 28, 29, 30, 36, 44, 54, 58